# ChromeBook
## SENIORS GUIDE

THE SIMPLEST CRASH COURSE FOR THE NON-TECH-SAVVY TO LEARN HOW TO USE YOUR CHROMEBOOK

**Nathan Chen**

# TABLE OF CONTENTS

# INTRODUCTION

If you're a Senior who just purchased a Chromebook, then you've come to the right place. Come along and let's discuss how to make the most of your Chromebook. Google's ChromeBook has undoubtedly been around for a while, but in comparison to the company's lineup of Android devices, it has largely been neglected. Google is finally giving this new computing platform the attention it deserves with the recent launch of ChromeBooks, and it will continue to grow rapidly in the years to come. The ChromeBook represents a new computer paradigm as well as a new line of laptops.

The safest operating system now in use is automatically updated and free of viruses and malware. The ChromeBook can accomplish practically anything that can be done by regular laptops by utilizing the power of the Internet. It has everything you require and nothing extra.

This book offers everything Seniors actually need to improve their ChromeBook experience, including setup instructions, tips, shortcuts and solutions for common problems. You can also take part in the Chromebook discussion if you're planning to purchase a new computer soon.

This book is written specially for the Seniors, keeping in mind their use-cases and requirements, so that they can have the optimum user experience while working with their Chromebooks

Let's get started!

CHAPTER 1

# A BRIEF HISTORY OF THE CHROMEBOOK

The Chromebook has really come into the limelight in the past few years. While there's still the traditional Apple Mac and Windows PC, the Chromebook is the device you want to try out if you don't need a full-fledged PC or laptop. At first glance, it looks like a normal laptop.

Actually, it is a normal laptop. There's really no difference in the look except for the fact that it's smaller than traditional laptops. But, even when they parade a relatively small body, everything is quite the same in the way they deliver services to the user. It's when you power it up and log in that you get to experience the whole new world you've never seen before. This is because of the OS, or operating system.

So the Chromebook is a laptop that runs on the Chrome OS rather than Windows or macOS. That's simple. But then, what is the Chrome OS? To come straight to the point, the Chrome OS is a twin of the Chrome browser. The Chrome browser can be downloaded on a Windows PC or Mac. But that's not all. The Chrome OS is not just a browser, it's way more.The Chromebook is great but there's something you should know. Since the operating system is different from Mac and Windows PC, you might not be able to use some of the applications that you have in your previous MacBook or Windows computer.

But if the app comes in a web form, you can access it with the browser. Another option is if there's a mobile app equivalent to the program. If the app has a mobile version, you can download it on the Chromebook and use it. But the question I asked myself is, how will a mobile app work on a laptop? This brings us to the next point.

Google owns Chrome, and also the Chrome OS. Actually they own a lot of things. But another thing they own is the Play Store. Yes, the Google Play Store that you have on your Android device. It's the place where you can download apps for your device. It's like the home of apps. So when Google was creating the Chrome OS, they made it capable of being compatible with the Play Store and its functions.

And that is why if an app is available in the Play Store, it's as good as already downloaded on your Chromebook. Chromebooks don't cost a leg and an arm unlike most traditional laptops. So getting one should not be hard if you run a tight budget. I do too.

The device largely depends on cloud storage to be used effectively. This might not make it very sweet to use for those without a steady internet connection.

What happens if you want to store a movie? You will need to transfer to the cloud. If you want to store documents? You will need to transfer to the cloud. How will you transfer to the cloud without the internet?

But thankfully, there's the availability of the normal inbuilt storage. The downside is that it can be a bit low - just 32 GB for most of the models, while some have double of that, at 64 GB. Normally when you sign up for Google Drive, you get free storage of 15 GB. But when you get a Chromebook, you are gifted with 100GB free storage for the first year. A nice way to compensate for the loss of hard physical storage, and we'll take it. Speaking for myself, I do take it, with thanks.

With respect to size, the Chromebook doesn't really measure up to the normal laptops. But something to keep in mind is that models of Chromebooks vary. While some models can be up to 12.3 inches, some are about 11.6 inches. The 12.3 inches model tends to be the most common one. Then if you do some more digging, you might be able to find a 14-inch laptop as some manufacturers still produce them.

As for the internal memory, the basic models have a RAM of 4GB which is pretty decent for daily use. If you would like to do a bit more multitasking, then 8GB and 16GB RAM options are also available. But a normal user of the Chromebook might not need that high a RAM to go about their everyday life.

## Different models, prices and specs

Chromebooks are available in a range of models, each offering different specifications and prices to suit various user requirements and budgets. Here's a summary of some popular models:

**Google Pixel book Go:**

Price: Starts at approximately $649

Specs: Features Intel Core processor, 8GB-16GB RAM, 128GB-256GB SSD storage, 13.3-inch Full HD or 4K display, lightweight design, and extended battery life.

**Samsung Chromebook Plus/Pro:**

Price: Typically ranges from $400 to $600

Specs: Equipped with Intel Celeron/Core m3 processor, 4GB-8GB RAM, 32GB-64GB eMMC storage, 12.3-inch QHD touch display (Plus) or 12.3-inch QHD touch display with built-in stylus (Pro), and a versatile 2-in-1 design.

**ASUS Chromebook Flip C434:**

Price: Usually around $550

Specs: Features Intel Core m3/i5 processor, 4GB-8GB RAM, 64GB-128GB eMMC storage, 14-inch Full HD touch display, sleek aluminium body, and a convertible 2-in-1 design.

**Acer Chromebook Spin 713:**

Price: Typically priced around $600

Specs: Equipped with Intel Core i5/i7 processor, 8GB-16GB RAM, 128GB-256GB SSD storage, 13.5-inch 2K Verti View display, MIL-STD-810G durability rating, and a convertible 2-in-1 design.

**HP Chromebook x360 14:**

Price: Usually priced around $500

Specs: Features Intel Core i3/i5 processor, 8GB RAM, 64GB eMMC storage, 14-inch Full HD touch display, B&O speakers, and a convertible 2-in-1 design.

**Lenovo Chromebook Flex 5:**

Price: Typically priced around $400

Specs: Equipped with Intel Core i3/i5 processor, 4GB-8GB RAM, 64GB eMMC storage, 13.3-inch Full HD touch display, backlit keyboard, and a convertible 2-in-1 design with optional stylus support.

It's important to understand that a chromebook is not one product. Rather, it is a type of compact laptop. And just like laptops are sold by different brands and are available in various sizes with different specifications, the same is true for chromebooks as well.

Some of the top brands for chromebooks are Samsung, Lenovo, Acer, HP, Dell and Asus. You should keep the following things in mind while selecting a chromebook: -

1. Processors - Ideally you want the latest 10th gen processor in your chromebook for fast processing.

2. Memory - depending on your usage, you should decide how much memory you would need. The most basic chromebook models start from 4GB RAM, while 8GB is the most preferred size. Heavy users should go for larger memory models.

3. Screen size and resolution

4. Local storage size

5. USB ports

6. Quality of display and speakers

These are just the broad pointers. There are many buying guides available online but the best thing is to speak to others who are using chromebooks or walk into a showroom where you can test different models of chromebooks to see which one you like best.

**Difference between chrome and chromium**

The disparity between Chrome and Chromium lies in their development and features. While Chrome is a web browser developed by Google that comes with additional proprietary features such as built-in Flash player and support for proprietary codecs, Chromium serves as the open-source project from which Chrome is derived, lacking these proprietary additions. In essence, Chrome is based on Chromium but includes Google's proprietary enhancements, whereas Chromium provides a more stripped-down, open-source browsing experience without these extra features.

### Buying a Chromebook

Most of the big box stores (BestBuy, Walmart, etc.) sell Chromebooks. You can find them on their websites, and you can find some actually in the store. You should definitely go and see them in the store. Hold them, type on the keyboards, and especially check out the screen. As we get older, our eyes are just not what they used to be. You may have to make a trade-off between a very lightweight Chromebook, and a screen that's big enough to read easily. But it's best to make that decision after seeing the screens in person, and holding up the laptops to see how easy they'll be to carry.

Purchasing a Chromebook involves selecting a device that suits your needs and budget. With various models available, it's important to consider factors such as performance, display quality, storage capacity, and price. Chromebooks come in a range of prices, from budget-friendly options to higher-end models with advanced features. It's essential to research different models, read reviews, and compare specifications to find the best fit for your requirements. Additionally, consider factors like battery life, portability, and connectivity options when making your decision. Once you've chosen a Chromebook, you can typically purchase it from retailers or online stores, ensuring you get a device that meets your expectations for functionality and affordability.

### Chromeboxes

We've mentioned Chromeboxes a couple of times. A Chromebox is exactly like a Chromebook, but it's more like a desktop than the Chromebook's laptop form. It's a box that sits on your desk, and you attach a regular keyboard, mouse, and screen to it just like you would to any laptop. Like any desktop, it's not portable. But, like any desktop, you can have any sort of keyboard and mouse that makes you happy. More importantly, you can have as big a monitor on it as you'd like. As we get older, that becomes more important than we sometimes want to admit!

### Pricing

You can buy Chromebooks and Chromeboxes for anywhere from about $150 to well over a thousand dollars. As with any computer, the more you spend, the more powerful the computer you can get such as features like higher RAM, faster processor, bigger hard drive, etc. Now that so many of us are living on limited budgets, we're tempted to spend as little as possible. Think about that for a minute, though. Spending a little more might mean a computer that lasts you longer, and is therefore cheaper in the long run.

CHAPTER 2

# KEYBOARD FUNCTIONS AND HOW TO USE TOUCHPAD/ SET UP MOUSE

The keyboard on a **Chromebook function** much like any conventional keyboard, equipped with keys for typing and navigation purposes. Meanwhile, the touchpad serves as the primary means of interacting with the screen, facilitating actions such as cursor movement, clicking, and scrolling. Should you wish to incorporate an external mouse, you can do so by either plugging it into one of the USB ports or connecting it wirelessly via Bluetooth settings. Once connected, the mouse operates akin to its functionality on other computing devices, enabling users to achieve finer control and precision in navigation tasks. Furthermore, users have the option to personalize their mouse experience by adjusting settings such as pointer speed and button configurations to suit their preferences.

## Set Up Remote Desktop

This is another important thing you need to know how to do on Chromebook. Do you own a couple of devices? It's not unusual in America to find people who own a Chromebook, a regular Windows or macOS laptop, and a PC of some sort that stays put at home.

Chromebook Remote Desktop tool makes life easy for you if you're juggling a couple of these devices. When properly set up, you can remotely connect and use your PC or MacBook on a Chromebook device from afar. This is how you get it done:

- Ensure you've installed Chrome web browser on all your devices.
- Go to chrome.google.com/webstore on your PC or MacBook.
- Find Chrome Remote Desktop. When you add the necessary extensions, you'll be asked for permissions.
- Click Add, then watch as the Remote Desktop app appears on your home screen.
- Click on the app to open it, and choose Continue. This takes you to a new page where more permissions will be required
- Select Allow process. And you're almost done.
- Go to My Computer and click Get started to reach a new page where you'd set up a PIN for remotely accessing your PC from Chromebook.

You may be wondering how to now remove the other devices when you need to do so. Well, it isn't rocket science.

Just launch the Remote Desktop app on Chromebook.

Choose Continue >> Allow access >> Enter PIN.

You'd able to work seamlessly on the PC or Mac as if they're right in front of you instead of a Chromebook.

## Clean Up With PowerWash

This third tip is important, but it's not what you do every other day. We're talking of your liberty to completely clean out your Google account and everything you have inside a Chromebook. Then, you can reformat it to make it brand new again. Just a couple of clicks can make it happen. You'll deploy a tool called PowerWash to achieve this feat.

To do that:

- Start by opening the Chrome browser on your Chromebook.
- Click on the three vertical dots in the upper right corner to open the Chrome menu.
- Choose "Settings" from the dropdown menu to enter the Chromebook's settings page.
- Once you're in the Settings page, you can find the PowerWash option in two ways:
  - **Using the Search Bar:** At the top of the Settings page, there's a search bar. Type "PowerWash" into this bar, and the search will direct you to the PowerWash option.
  - **Via Advanced Settings:** If you prefer navigating through the menu, scroll down on the Settings page and click on "Advanced" to expand more options. Continue scrolling to the bottom of the Advanced section until you find the "Reset settings" area, where the PowerWash option is located.
- Next to the PowerWash entry, you'll see a button or a link that says "Reset" or "PowerWash." Click on it. A new window or dialog box will appear, confirming that you want to proceed with the PowerWash.
- Read the information carefully, as it will warn you that all data on your Chromebook will be erased. This includes all the accounts, files, and settings.
- If you're ready to proceed, confirm your choice. Depending on your device, you might need to click a button labeled "Restart," "Reset," or "PowerWash." The device will reboot and start the PowerWash process.

- After the PowerWash is complete, your Chromebook will restart as if it were new. You'll need to go through the initial setup process, which includes connecting to Wi-Fi, accepting the terms of service, and logging in with a Google account.

Watch as your Chromebook goes off and reboots, now looking as blank as it was the day you unboxed it.

## Send Files to Google Drive

As we noted earlier, Chrome OS devices generally come with limited internal storage space. But Google gives all users 15GB free storage on their drive. In fact, as an incentive to new Chromebook users, you'd get free 100GB for one year, to store the world, if you must.

For Chrome to save up downloaded files straight on Google drive without your prompting, you need to set some things up:

- Open the Chrome browser on your Chromebook.
- Click on the three dots in the upper right corner to open the Chrome menu.
- From the dropdown menu, select "Settings." This will take you to the Chrome settings page.
- Within the Settings page, scroll down and click on "Advanced" to expand the advanced settings options.
- In the Advanced settings section, look for the "Downloads" subsection. This area controls where your files are saved by default when you download them from the internet.
- In the Downloads subsection, you'll find an option labeled "Location" with a button or link next to it that says "Change." Click on this "Change" link.
- A window will pop up, allowing you to select a new default location for your downloads. Here, you can choose your Google Drive or a specific folder within your Google Drive as the default location. Navigate through the options and select either the Google Drive root or a particular folder within it.

- After selecting the desired location in your Google Drive, click "Open" or "Select" (the exact wording may vary) to confirm your choice.
- Go back to the Downloads subsection in the Chrome settings.
- You will see a checkbox or a toggle next to the option that says "Ask where to save each file before downloading." Make sure this option is unchecked or turned off. This step is crucial because leaving this option enabled will prompt you for a download location every time, overriding the default location you just set.
- Your changes are typically saved automatically, but you can close the Settings tab to ensure all settings are applied.

Your settings will be saved and any time you download something from the web, it defaults to your Google cloud storage.

**Steps to Get Bonus Google Drive Cloud Space**

You just heard that you can secure 100GB to store files on the cloud as a Chromebook user. It's real, but you won't get it automatically.

Look up Chromebook.com/goodies to view what's on display at the moment. Freebies might include music, movies etc.

- Get down to Google Drive and see that there's indeed 100GB storage space for you in there.
- Click Redeem offer and wait a moment. You'll be prompted to allow the system to verify if your device is qualified for the freebie space.
- Click yes to allow for compatibility checks.
- Then expect a positive announcement that you've redeemed free cloud storage that makes up for perceived low capacity in Chromebook tech devices.

**Accessing Google Drive on Offline Mode**

Being able to do things in the offline mode is an advantage, especially when you're on board an airplane and have your device on airplane mode.

There may be other reasons for not being able to connect to a wireless network at a time. It's good to know that you can continue doing certain work offline, if only you're properly set up.

Here's what you need to do to enjoy Google Office Suite offline:

- In My Drive, click on the gear icon and select Settings
- Tick inside the box aligned with the option Sync Google Docs, Sheets etc, so you can edit them offline
- After you check the right box, you're good to go.

Anything you create, edit or modify offline will be synchronized automatically when next you go online.

## Adjust Screen Resolution

It's said that Chromebooks won't win competition for best display screens in the world. This isn't saying that they're terrible. No, they aren't.

We're just saying you may need to adjust your screen resolution for one reason or the other.

If you see reasons to fine-tune your screen,

- Click on Settings >> Display settings, then adjust your resolution manually.
- Don't forget the standard image magnification tools on the Chrome browser. These also enable you to refit anything on the Chromebook screen.
- You can find the zoom tool on the menu, or use the shortcuts, which we advised that you spend time to master.
- Use Ctrl + plus to increase an image, and use Ctrl + minus to reduce it. Ctrl + 0 (this is zero, not letter 'o') will revert your image to original size.

## Use Smartphone to Unlock Chromebook

Enabling the "Smart Lock" feature on a Chromebook allows users to unlock their device using their smartphone. To set this up, users must first ensure that both their

Chromebook and smartphone are signed in to the same Google account and have Bluetooth enabled. Then, they need to navigate to the Chromebook's settings menu, select "Connected devices," and turn on the "Smart Lock" feature. After enabling Smart Lock, users must follow the on-screen instructions to pair their smartphone with the Chromebook via Bluetooth. Once paired, the Chromebook will automatically detect the presence of the paired smartphone and remain unlocked when it's nearby and unlocked itself. In case the smartphone moves out of range or locks, the Chromebook will prompt the user to enter their password or use another authentication method to regain access. Additionally, users can quickly lock their Chromebook by pressing the Search + L shortcut keys simultaneously, ensuring security when they step away from their device. This integration of smartphone and Chromebook enhances user convenience by providing a seamless unlocking experience while maintaining security measures.

## Getting Dropbox into Chromebook

You may not be aware that your Dropbox can be integrated with your storage system on Chromebook. There's an app that can help you to do that. It's called File System for Dropbox.

- Just download it from the Chrome OS app store
- Give it whatever permissions it needs, or the ones you think it should have on your device.
- Open the app and click on Mount.
- Enter your Dropbox details.
- You're good to go, as the new storage item will now show on the left side of the file manager.

### Third Party Domain Name Server on Chromebook

As you may know, domain name servers are the address book or directory lodged on the internet. While using your Chromebook, it is easy to locate and use any third party server you want to use.

Maybe you want a more secure domain, or you need to get around a content block, or just a faster service, this is how you get a third party Internet Protocol (IP) address:

- Open Settings
- Click on the domain name you're changing. In the window that follows, select network.
- Look down the bottom of the tab and choose your new IP address from the options provided. If you have one in mind, you can enter it manually.
- On the new server, you may just be able to surf faster or even bypass any content block your former network provider might have put in your way.

## Use Overview Mode

Overview Mode on a Chromebook allows users to view all open windows and applications at a glance, facilitating multitasking and efficient navigation. To enter Overview Mode, users can press the Overview key, typically located on the top row of the keyboard and represented by a square or rectangle icon. Alternatively, they can use the shortcut key combination of the Overview key along with the "F5" or "F6" key. Once in Overview Mode, users can see thumbnails of all open windows and applications, arranged in a grid-like layout. They can then click on a thumbnail to switch to that window or application, making it easy to switch between tasks quickly. Additionally, users can drag and drop windows to rearrange them or swipe up on the touchpad with three fingers to enter Overview Mode. Exiting Overview Mode is as simple as clicking on any window or pressing the Overview key again. This feature enhances productivity by providing a convenient way to manage multiple tasks simultaneously on a Chromebook.

Here are the steps to use Overview Mode on a Chromebook:

- Ensure that you have multiple windows or applications open on your Chromebook.
- Press the "Overview" key, which is typically located on the top row of the keyboard and resembles a square or rectangle icon. Alternatively, you can use

the shortcut key combination of the Overview key along with the "F5" or "F6" key.

- Once in Overview Mode, you'll see thumbnails of all open windows and applications arranged in a grid-like layout.
- Click on a thumbnail to switch to the corresponding window or application. This allows you to easily navigate between different tasks.
- If needed, you can drag and drop windows to rearrange them within Overview Mode.
- Alternatively, you can swipe up on the touchpad with three fingers to enter Overview Mode.
- To exit Overview Mode, simply click on any window or press the Overview key again. This will return you to your selected window or application.

## Deploy SSD Card as Permanent Storage

To deploy an SSD card as permanent storage on your Chromebook, you can follow these steps:

- First, ensure your Chromebook is powered off. Insert the SSD card into the appropriate slot on your Chromebook. The location of the slot may vary depending on the model of your Chromebook.
- Once the SSD card is securely inserted, power on your Chromebook and log in to your account.
- Click on the system tray located in the bottom-right corner of the screen, then click on the gear icon to access the Settings menu.
- In the Settings menu, navigate to the "Device" section and select "Storage."
- Locate the SSD card listed under the "External storage" section. Click on it and then select the option to format the SSD card. Follow the on-screen prompts to complete the formatting process. Be aware that formatting the SSD card will erase any existing data on it.
- After formatting, you'll be given the option to set up the SSD card as permanent storage. Follow the prompts to complete this setup process.

- Once the SSD card is set up as permanent storage, you can start transferring files to it. You can do this by simply dragging and dropping files from your Chromebook's internal storage to the SSD card in the Files app.

By following these steps, you can effectively deploy an SSD card as permanent storage on your Chromebook, providing additional space for storing files and expanding the capabilities of your device.

## Share the Chromebook Safely

While discussing the setup process, we saw that other users can share the Chromebook with you, each logging in with their respective Google accounts. But you still need to protect yourself. You need to ensure that the sharing does not compromise your personal information and files.

- So, on your lock screen,
- Hit the Sign Out button on the bottom left side. You're out.
- Leave the device on guest user mode.

Another user can then log in with his Google identities. They will not access anything on your account. But the record of their activities on Google Chrome gadgets will synchronize in your Chromebook.

But, you need not be alarmed. Since the guest user signed in on guest mode, everything they did on your Chromebook will automatically be erased when they sign out.

What if you prefer not to share with anyone? Or you want to restrict sharing to just one or two persons. There's a way to do that.

Go to Settings >> Users >> restrict users to specific accounts.

## Get Your Calculations Done

To get your calculations done efficiently on a Chromebook, you can utilize the built-in calculator app or Google Sheets, Google's spreadsheet application, which includes robust calculation capabilities. To access the calculator app, simply click on the

Launcher icon located in the bottom-left corner of the screen and search for "Calculator." Alternatively, you can use Google Sheets by opening the app from the Launcher or accessing it through the Google Drive website. Once you're in the calculator app or Google Sheets, you can perform various calculations, including basic arithmetic, complex formulas, and data analysis. Use the keyboard shortcuts such as "+" for addition, "-" for subtraction, "*" for multiplication, and "/" for division to input calculations quickly. Additionally, Google Sheets supports a wide range of functions and formulas, which you can find in the "Functions" menu or by typing "=" followed by the function name. For example, "=SUM (A1:A10)" calculates the sum of cells A1 to A10. After entering your calculations, press Enter to get the results instantly. With these tools and shortcuts, you can streamline your calculations and increase your productivity on your Chromebook.

## Taking Screenshots

This isn't a tough job, neither on Chromebook nor in any modern device that you've come across. You can always capture and save the picture, illustration or chat thread that you fancy so much. And you wish to keep it or show it to another colleague.

- Press the control key down and hit the task switch key, the same one with the sign of multiple open windows above the number 6 key.
- After capturing the screen, expect a notification.
- Click on the notification to view what you snapped. It'll get stored in your Files app.

## Take a Look at Chromebook System Info

Do you really need to see all that technical information about your Chromebook loaded in the graphical user interface, or GUI?

Let's assume that you've more than the run of the mill knowledge of these things, and you'd like to know everything about the CPU, the processors, the memory, and everything else besides. This is what you do:

- Go to Omnibox,
- Enter chrome://system to access the graphical user interface.
- Here, the system info is deftly arranged and easy to read. You can learn as much as you're capable of learning about your device here.

### Quick Access to the Launcher

On a normal day, you do not find it hard to get to the Chrome OS launcher. But there's a way to even do it faster.

The quick access is especially useful if you're using a Chromebook tablet.

Just swipe up from any empty space at the bottom of your screen. Hurray, the launcher is there staring at you!

## Hide Chromebook Shelf

Yeah, you can hide that row of icons that show your favorites. You find this nestled at the bottom part of your Chromebook screen.

- Just a right click, or a long-press if you prefer. And you'd see options of what to do with the shelf.
- Well, you'd like to hide it. So, select Auto Hide and watch as the shelf disappears.

### Clear Notifications

In Android OS, you can clear a bunch of notifications with a mere click on one button. This is also possible on the Chromebook.

The downside is, you may not easily find this option on Chrome OS devices.

Not until you scroll down to the bottom of your screen, past the oldest notification.

Then, you'd see the Clear All option. Select this button and enjoy the satisfaction of uncluttering your space.

CHAPTER 3

# HOW TO SETUP CHROMEBOOK FOR THE FIRST TIME

## Connect To Power

Connecting your Chromebook to power is a straightforward process that ensures your device remains charged for optimal use. Begin by locating the power adapter that came with your Chromebook and the power outlet you plan to use. Next, insert the power plug into the charging port on your Chromebook. It's typically located on the side or rear of the device. Once the plug is securely inserted, plug the other end of the power adapter into the power outlet. You may hear a faint click when the connection is secure. A charging indicator light on your Chromebook should illuminate, indicating that it's receiving power. As your Chromebook charges, you can continue using it or leave it to charge uninterrupted. To check the battery level while charging, click on the status area in the bottom-right corner of the screen. You'll see the battery icon, which displays the current battery level. Additionally, pressing Alt + Shift + S will show detailed system information, including battery status, ensuring you're aware of your Chromebook's power status at all times. By following these steps and using shortcuts, you can easily connect your Chromebook to power and ensure it remains charged for your computing needs.

## Login to Google

The next thing to do is to login into your Google account. You should be able to do this as soon as your Chromebook turns on. You might think that the process of signing in might be a bit harder or takes longer than normal but actually it is none of those.

You should have a Google account by now. (And if you don't, create one like right now). So you should be used to signing in to your Gmail account or Google account. You know the process. It’s just same as trying to sign in to your Chromebook. When you're signed in, you will be able to access your themes, settings, bookmarks and other features from your Google account.

## Connect To Wi-Fi

To connect your Chromebook to a Wi-Fi network, start by clicking on the network icon located in the bottom right corner of the screen. This will open a list of available Wi-Fi networks. Select the network you want to connect to and enter the password if prompted. Once the correct password is entered, your Chromebook will automatically connect to the Wi-Fi network, allowing you to browse the internet and access online services.

## Download Some Apps

With your Chromebook, you have access to the Google Play store. And to be honest, this is a blessing. I say this because the Chromebook and Android are best friends. So if you have an Android game that you downloaded on the Play Store for your Android device, you can be sure that you'll be able to download that same game on your Chromebook.

But, while this is true for many of the apps you should note that it is not all. Not all apps can be installed on the Chrome OS. But most of them should. You can download apps like Lightroom, Microsoft Word, Netflix, Amazon video, comiXology and all your favorite apps on your Chromebook.

And in fact when you do download them, they'll take your Chromebook experience to the next level. So don't just stop at the basic apps you get on your Chromebook. Reach for the sky.

## Test Out the Touchpad

You can go ahead and connect your wireless or wired mouse to your Chromebook. But before you do, you should definitely check out the touchpad.

Check to see if the touchpad is working. It is fantastic and easy to use on the Chromebook.

The best part about the Chromebook touchpad is that it has full gesture support. But if you've been using some kind of laptop that doesn't support that, you don't have to worry. In a short while, you'll get used to it and you will be using it like a pro.

CHAPTER 4

# HOW TO SETUP AND USE THE GOOGLE SUITE PRODUCTIVITY TOOLS

## Productivity with Google Suite

Setting up and using Google Suite productivity tools is a seamless process that offers a wide range of features for efficient work. To begin, ensure you have a Google account, which provides access to Google Drive, Docs, Sheets, and Slides. Start by navigating to the Google Drive website or launching the Google Drive app on your device. Here, you can create new documents, spreadsheets, or presentations by clicking on the "+" button or selecting the desired file type from the "New" menu. Alternatively, you can access these tools directly by visiting their respective websites or opening the corresponding apps. Once you've created a document, spreadsheet, or presentation, you can begin editing and formatting it using the toolbar at the top of the screen. Use keyboard shortcuts like Ctrl + C for copy, Ctrl + V for paste, and Ctrl + B for bold to expedite your workflow. Additionally, collaborate with others in real-time by sharing files and granting them editing or viewing permissions. To do this, click on the "Share" button and enter the email addresses of the collaborators. They will receive an invitation to access the document and can begin collaborating immediately. With these steps and shortcuts, you can harness the power of Google Suite productivity tools to streamline your work and enhance collaboration with others.

## Getting Around Google Docs

Google Docs is a word processor that is essential in making your document or text unique. Google Docs makes it possible for you to format, edit, and create documents online. Editing the document with someone else is also possible on Google Docs. You can also work with your colleagues on Google Docs through instant messaging and videos. Google Docs does not have all the functions that are found in Microsoft Word but it’s still loaded with quite a few features that make it useful.

## Using Paragraph Styles

You can use the following paragraph styles to format and update your documents quickly and easily. The paragraph styles are also used on titles, regular paragraphs, and headings.

Heading: To change the text style on your heading, go to Google Docs and open the document you want to work on. Choose the text to be changed. Then click Format and you will see the paragraph styles. The paragraph styles will be written Normal text, Title, Subtitle, and Heading 1 up to 6. Select the style you want and click Apply and your heading will change to the style you have selected.

Bold, italic, and underlined: Choose the text to be modified, then go to the shortcut toolbar. Click the bold (B), italic (I), or underline (U) buttons and you will visibly see the change as per your selection.

Changing fonts: Highlight the text that you want to change. Then go to the toolbar and click where it is written Font size. The list of all the font sizes will appear and you choose the one you want to use like 12 (GCF Global, n.d). Your text will change its size either to become bigger or smaller depending on your new selection.

Font color: To change the font color, select the text to be altered first. Tap the Text color option from the toolbar and a menu of colors will appear as circles. Click on the circle with the color you want and it will be applied to your text. For example, if you choose the red circle, your selected text will automatically become red.

## Justify Text

Look for the four parallel lines of the same size on the task toolbar and tap on them. Once you select that symbol, all the text you are going to type will be justified. Your text will be evenly distributed between the margins and you will achieve a clean document . You can also justify a block of text. Highlight the block of text to be justified first and then do the procedure explained in this paragraph.

You can also justify the text using a keyboard shortcut. Press the Ctrl + Shift + J simultaneously and the text you selected will be justified.

## Bullet Lists

Open the document in Google Docs on your Chromebook and click the page or text to which you want to add the bullets. Check for three parallel lines with dots at the beginning of each line on the toolbar. Once you click the symbol, you will have bullets that are like black dots. Click the arrow on that symbol for more suggestions on the types of bullets to use. Then click on the one you prefer and it will be created on your document.

## Numbered Lists

There is a symbol on the toolbar that has three numbered parallel lines. Go to that symbol and click on it. Your text or document will be numbered and for more numbering formats, click on the arrow besides the lines. Choose the numbering format you want and it will be applied to your document.

## Cut, Copy, and Paste

When copying or cutting text or document, you are saving it temporarily in a Clipboard until you paste it somewhere else where it will be used. Cutting is when removing the document from its original place to another and copying is making a duplicate.

So to cut or copy, highlight the text or the whole document you want. Click the Edit option on the toolbar and you will see the drop-down menu. Select copy or cut and the information will be stored shortly in the clipboard. Go to the page or document where you want to place the text and click Edit again. On the appearing menu, select paste or press Ctrl + V on the keyboard at the same time. Your text will be placed in the new location.

## Adding Images

Start by opening your presentation or document. Afterwards, click Insert, then Image. More options on where to get the image will pop-up and you have to choose the right one. For example, there will be options like Drive, upload from computer, or by URL. Lastly, click on the insert or open option and your image will be placed where you want it to be.

## Adding Tables

Open the page where you want to add the table. Select the exact spot where to add the table in your document by placing the cursor. After that, click the Insert symbol on the task toolbar, then select Table. After that, choose the size of the table you want. The size of the table is determined by the number of rows and columns you need.

There is also another option to add or delete rows and columns in case of miscalculations. Do the right-click on your table and the options on how to insert, delete, sort, and distribute the rows and columns will be available for you. Then, you can choose accordingly.

## Saving Documents

You can save your Google Doc as a Word or PDF document on your Chromebook. Look for File at the left top corner of your device's toolbar and click it. Then move the cursor to Download and select the file type in which you will download the document from the list on the menu. Choose PDF or Microsoft Word to save your Google Docs according to your preferences.

If you are using a mobile phone, check for the three dots at the top right side and press them. You will see a drop-down list of options. Select Share and Export, then Save As. Afterward, you need to choose the type of file for your download from the options. Now, you can press Ok and then tap on .docx (Word) or PDF to save your Google Doc according to your preferences. Your documents are now saved.

You can also save the Google Doc to Google Drive but you need to activate Ask first so that you can save the file prior to downloading Google Drive directly to your device.

## Opening Saved Documents

To open your saved documents, log into your Google account on drive.google.com using your username and password. You should know how to regain your password or username if you can't remember it. Then, double click the file where you saved the documents and open the one you want. The document will open using your Google account despite it being a slide presentation, form, or Google Doc. The audio files, photos, videos, and PDFs open using the Google drive.

You can also use other applications you installed on your device or web apps to open the files. If you are using the installed apps, make sure you have the Application Launcher and a current version of the Backup and Sync by Google. If you meet all the requirements then you can go to drive.google.com and log into your account.

Remember to keep your username and password in mind. On a file, do the right-click and move your cursor to Open with and select the application of your choice to open your saved document. Make sure you have a default app that is specifically for opening other types of files .

## Printing Documents

It is possible for you to print a Google Doc on a wireless or wired printer. So to print the document, go to Google Docs. Select and open the document you want to print and go to the top left corner of your device's screen and check for File. Click on that and you will find Print on the menu. Click on it. You will see a window that looks like your page. You should find your printer and select it, but sometimes it might not appear on the list. If that happens, click on See More to search for your printer and get connected to it. Once you get your printer, click on the Print button that will be blue in color.

Printing a document on Google Docs from your mobile phone can be done if you have the Google Docs app on your device. Gain access to the document by signing in to the relevant account. Select the document you want to print and press the three dot icon that will be on the top right side of your screen. Many drop-down options will appear and you should choose Share and Export. By clicking on it, another menu will pop-up and that's where you will find Print. Selecting the Print option will lead you to the window where you are supposed to choose the printer to use. Upon printer selection, you go on to tap on another Print symbol and your document will start printing.

When printing, remember to select the number of copies to be printed and how the document will look like on paper such as portrait or landscape mode.

## Sharing Documents

When sharing Google Docs, access your Google Drive by typing https://drive.google.com in a web browser. You can also sign in to your Google Docs account. Then, click on the file you are willing to share to open it. Your document is now open. Check for the blue Share button at the upper-right corner of your document. Click on it and start adding your recipients. Type every recipient's name or the group's name and add it by tapping on it when it appears. If the person or group is not using Google Docs, once you enter their names they are going to receive an invite. The invite will instruct them to generate a free account so that they can access the document sent to them.

Once you click on the recipient's name, the sharing permissions will appear. From the list, you can decide if the people you are sharing the document with can comment, view, or edit the document. For example, if you want the person to only view the document, select Viewer. Check also for more advanced settings by clicking on the tab that is on the top-right corner of your toolbar. By doing this, you will be allowing the recipient like the commenter or viewer to copy, print, or download the document. The editor will also be given the right to share the document with other people or to also change permissions.

Now, you are done with sharing permissions, check the box for Notify People if you are sending via email. Verify that there is a checkmark in the box next to the Notify People option. If you want the recipients to receive a notification that you have shared a document with them, check the box and leave a text in the Message box to give more details about the document. Then, click Notify so that your receiver can get an email with a link for them to access the document.

If you don't want them to receive the notification, remove the checkmark. Your document is now ready to be shared so click on Send and the recipient will have access to it.

## Google Sheets

Google sheets is also a Workspace that is web-based where you can do collaborations, chat, and create videos as a team. There is no limit on the size of the group. The application allows the users to perform different tasks like sharing the data in real time online, updating, modifying, and creating spreadsheets. Google sheets are crucial as you can see the changes while happening, receive notifications for edits that were done in your absence, and also add collaborators easily to projects. The changes you make on your Google Sheets are automatically saved. You can also sort, delete, and add rows and columns on Google Sheets.

## Spreadsheets

A Spreadsheet is also known as a worksheet. This file is created through a combination of rows and columns that enable you to calculate numerical data, arrange, organize, and sort data perfectly. Having a spreadsheet has its own benefit as you will be able to do mathematical calculations of the data in the cells using the formulas.

## Getting Around Google Sheets

Google Sheets plays an important role by making the work of every department easier as you can prepare the invoices, create lists, makedo budgets, and analyze statistical data. When using Google Sheets, you can work with a variety of functions on your documents and some of them are discussed below.

## Simple Text Formatting

Text formatting can be done by changing the font size, color, alignment, font appearance, and font name. Font appearance involves italic, underline, background font cell color, and bold.

## Cut, Copy, and Paste

The procedure for copying and cutting is the same. The only difference is that when copying, you are creating a duplicate of the original while cutting is when you move the data to a new location. So to copy the cell contents, start by choosing the cell with the data you want. Then, check for Edit on the toolbar and on the drop-down list, choose Copy or you can press Ctrl + C at the same time and the contents will be copied. Go on to select the cell where you want to paste the contents. Click Edit again and select Paste from the list. You can also do the shortcut by pressing Ctrl + V concurrently to paste the data in the new cell.

## Inserting Rows and Columns

Start by opening the spreadsheets. Next, select the column or row where you want to insert another one. After that, click on the Insert tab and there will be options for you to choose if you are inserting the Row above or below. If you are to choose the columns, it's either Column right or Column left. By clicking on your selection, you will automatically have a column or row where you want it to be.

## Cell Alignment

You can align the cell either vertically or horizontally. Click on Vertical align or Horizontal align depending on your choice and finally choose alignment. Your cell will be aligned accordingly.

## Cell Borders

First thing is to open your spreadsheet and then select the cells in which you want to add borders. Then click Borders. There will be a list of borders available for selection so you choose the type of border you wish to put on your cell. You can also choose the Border style and Border color so that your cell borders have the specific lines and color that you like. You are now through with all the stages involved and should be able to see your choice of borders.

## Using Formulas

You should pick the cell in which you want to have the calculated value. For example, the cell in which you are going to put the total value after calculating. Type the equal sign (=) in the selected cell and then write the cell address after the equal sign. For example, suppose you want to reference the cell C10 first in the formula. Continue to put the operator you want to use, for example the minus sign (-). Type the second reference cell address for example, C12 and tap on Enter on the keyboard. Your results will be displayed in the cell where you put the formula. To prove if the formula is working, change the value of the cell address. Your result should also change.

## Using Functions

You should know how to use Functions from the toolbar because it is easy and fast. Pick the cell where you want the calculated result to be and go on to select Functions. A menu of five functions will pop-up and there will be submenus that have every possible function. Finally, select the cells you wish to put in the range and press Enter. Note that when choosing the cells, press and hold Ctrl and make your choices if you are selecting individual cells. Press and hold Shift and choose the initial and last cells in the range for a continuous selection.

## Count

Type the equals sign in the cell for the formula. Type C from your keyboard and you will have a list of options, then choose Count. Put the open bracket and write the cell address to be involved, then close the bracket. Press Enter to get your result.

AutoSum

AutoSum is a built-in intelligent function that works automatically by predicting the range for which you want to do the calculation. Place the cursor on the result cell for, say, E15 and press AutoSum. The spreadsheet will automatically give you the sum of E2:E14.

## Types of Data

Texts and numbers are common types of data in Google Sheets although there is another one called Boolean values. Boolean values include errors, arrays, and true or false. The TYPE function can be used to detect the type of data if you are not certain of what is in the cell.

## Adding Charts

Click on your Google Sheet to open it. Do the selection of cells you are willing to use in the chart. If you do not have a Google Sheet, go to sheets.new and generate it. Do cell selection by clicking on the first one while holding shift. Keep holding while choosing the other cells to be included, then tap Insert and further select Chart from the options. Your chart will be added and by default, the Google Sheet will choose the chart for you using the data you have provided. To customize the chart, choose from the menu that will appear to your right when you click Chart.

## Insert Table

Have a spreadsheet with tabular data on it and format it by doing the center alignment and bolding. You should also remember to freeze the header row while in the sheet's first row so that you will always see it when scrolling. Then, filter the rows by tapping on Data and choose Create filter, leaving the row for totals unfiltered. Filtering will aid in easy identification of important data. Make sure you apply Indirect Function so that the totals can update automatically whenever there are new columns and rows.

Give your table an identity for easy referencing wherever you use it. Have a name range that will include the header row. Your table is ready to be tested by entering a certain number of rows.

## Google Slides

Google Slides is an online application that can be used for creating new and editing old templates. Google Slides serve the same purpose as PowerPoint. The difference with Google Slides is that you can access your presentation on any device and from wherever you are as long as it was saved on the Google cloud. The changes can also be auto-saved and all the users can have access to Google Sides and work on the presentation simultaneously.

You should know how to use Google Slides for your personal benefit or for your business. Here are some of the functions you can perform on Google Slides to make your presentation better.

## Designing a Slide

On the top right side of your Google's home page, there is a grid. Click on it and then go to Drive on the menu. You can also log in to https://slides.google.com to quickly get the Slides page. Look for the blue tab and tap it so that you can select Google Slides on the menu to open a slide page. On the toolbar, find a (+) to create a new slide. Give your slide a name and a theme of your choice.

## Slide Layer Arrangement

Open your presentation and click on the object you want to move. Select Arrange followed by Order. Finally, choose the option that is best for you.

## Add a New Slide

You can add a new slide to the existing presentation by opening the Google Drive and tap the Google Slides presentation you are to add a slide. Choose the slide you like from the left column and click Insert and New slide. You now have a new slide in your presentation.

## Change Slide Layout

The text and images' arrangement can be changed. Begin by opening the Google Slides presentation and pick a slide. Look at the top of your device and click Layout, prior to selecting your favorite layout to apply to the presentation.

## Slide Masters

On your toolbar, select View and then Slide Master. Change the color, styles, alignment, and text but you can also choose Theme before all the changes to the presentation. Click Close Master View once you've completed all the other stages.

## Slide Transitions

Look for the slide sorter view at the bottom of your device's screen. The thumbnails of all the slides will appear on the Google Sheet. Click on Transitions and the group Transition to This Slide will show up giving you the opportunity to choose the current effect to be used when the transition is taking place.

## Slide Animations

On the Animation tab, find the Advanced Animation group and click on the Animation Pane. The animation options appear on the pane. Click Add Animation and you need to apply the effects to four options that include motion, emphasis, exit, and entrance. You can now select a slide and add the animation you like and the results will be seen on the Slide pane. The animations will permit you to control how the objects or text should appear on the slide. Speed adjustments can also be done on the speed box.

## Add an Image

Go to your Google Slides presentation and select the slide to add an image on it. Click Insert, then go on to look for an image by either searching from the Web or to choose from the ones already there in your device. Select the image from the options. Double-click to add the image and you are done.

## Resize an Image

The size of the image on your presentation can be adjusted to a larger or smaller size. First, highlight the image by clicking on it. On the squares that are on the edges of your image, press and hold the left-mouse button. Drag the mouse away or toward the image to increase or decrease its size.

## Crop an Image

To begin, open the slide so that you can choose the image to crop. Find the crop button on the screen or double-click on the image. You can use the black lines on the image to adjust the cropping by dragging them. Once you finish the adjustments, tap again on the Crop or Enter to complete the process.

## Add a Video

Create a new Google Slide presentation or open an old one on slides.google.com. Start by clicking on Insert and then select Video. Find the search tab and type the title or any word that can lead to a successful search of the video you wish to add. Tap on

Enter to command the search process. Once your video appears on the list, select it and it will be added to your slide. You can resize and reposition the video on the presentation. Use the blue dots on the corners and sides of your slide to do that.

## Add a Chart

Your slide should be open so that you can select the slide in which you want to insert your chart. Click Insert then Chart and it will be available on your presentation.

## Printing Presentations

Open the presentation to be printed. Select the part to be printed—either the whole presentation or particular slides. Click on File and select Print from the menu. If you are printing the entire sheet, click on the workbook. Also, click on Current sheet if you selected the sheet to print and Selected cells if you are printing chosen cells only.

## Sharing Your Presentation

You should open your presentation first. Click on the spreadsheet and select option Share and add emails of the recipients. Click on the down arrow so that you can set the permissions and if you send a notification, remember to give a brief information about the spreadsheet you sent. After everything, tap Send and the recipient can now access it. If you are giving the link, just click on Share, then Copy Link. You will get the link from Get link and paste it on other users' emails.

## Present With Chromecast

Chromecast enables you to present the spreadsheet on another device using wireless screen sharing, as it is powered by Bluetooth. If you are a chrome browser user, you can cast a tab that contains the Google Slides, Sheets, and Docs so that you can use it when conducting meetings. A Chromecast uses power and the HDMI to connect to the projector or TV. It also uses Wi-Fi network to perform its functions.

If you want to present with Chromecast, open the information you wish to present.

Tap on Google cast extension so that your tab can be casted to the Chromecast.

CHAPTER 5

# MUST HAVE APPS TO INTERACT WITH OTHERS AND HOW TO SET THEM UP

## Google Meet

Google Meet is a video conferencing app that allows you to connect with others through video calls. To set it up, simply visit the Google Meet website or install the Google Meet app from the Chrome Web Store. Sign in with your Google account, and you can start or join video meetings with ease.

## Google Hangouts

Google Hangouts is a messaging and video call app that integrates seamlessly with your Google account. To use it, simply open the Hangouts website or app, sign in with your Google account, and start messaging or making video calls to your contacts.

## Zoom

Zoom is a popular video conferencing app that offers a range of features for virtual meetings and webinars. To set it up, visit the Zoom website or install the Zoom app from the Chrome Web Store. Sign up for an account or sign in with your existing account, and you can start hosting or joining Zoom meetings.

## Microsoft Teams

Microsoft Teams is a collaboration platform that offers chat, video conferencing, file sharing, and more. To set it up, visit the Microsoft Teams website or install the Microsoft Teams app from the Chrome Web Store. Sign in with your Microsoft account or your organization's account, and you can start collaborating with your team members.

## Astro file browser

This is one popular app that comes with an inbuilt app manager that will allow you to see the file's size and the day it was last opened. The file manager part of the app will allow you to list the files according to their type, like videos, music, pictures. If you have some files stored in the cloud, the Astro app covers Dropbox, Google drive, Microsoft OneDrive, Facebook and Box.

## Discord

The discord app will mostly be used by gamers. It's just like IRC and you can connect to a server then engage in some private chat rooms. The discord app allows you to be connected to several servers at the same time and you can then choose a server and look into each room if there are any new messages.

## Dropbox

With the Dropbox app, you get access to a place where you can store all of your photos, files or videos. You can get access to Dropbox with the app and sign in to your Dropbox account. And this gives a ridiculous amount of free storage space. And since the Chromebook is a device with small hard drive, you will depend heavily on cloud based storage service like Dropbox

## Files by Google

An amazing tool created by Google for the main purpose of cleaning android phones. The home screen of the app will show your recently accessed files in several categories. You can also use this app to clear out any unwanted app.

## Firefox Focus

The Mozilla Firefox browser doesn't work with Chromebooks like the Acer Chromebook 13. But an option that worked is the Firefox Focus. This one gives you more privacy and security as ads are blocked. You can also block cookies, embedded videos, web fonts and others manually.

## Gmail offline

If you would like to be fed with your latest emails without needing internet connection, the Gmail offline app is the way to go. You will have your messages synced with the Gmail offline app when you are connected so that when you are offline, you have the mails waiting for you to peruse. This is very helpful when you are in the subway or on an airplane. Another cool thing is that you can type your reply if you would like to reply to the sender and the app will store it. When you happen to have the slightest hint of an internet connection, the app sends it.

## IHeartRadio

For those who want to listen to live local broadcasting series, the IHeartRadio app is a great option. This also streams different stations from around the nation and you can hear channels that are based on bands or artists. The android version of this app is simple and easy to navigate.

## Microsoft Office

If you don't want to use the Google Docs and are determined to use Microsoft oOffice apps, then you'll be happy to know that Microsoft Word, Outlook, PowerPoint and Excel are available for android. Which means you can use them on your Chromebook. You will be able to perform some basic tasks like creating a spreadsheet with Excel or writing a document with Word.

## Minecraft

As you know, this list will not be complete without mentioning Minecraft. The android version of the apps works perfectly on the Chrome OS and it even supports touchscreen, keyboards or gamepads. If you are already a Minecraft fan, there's really nothing new to see. You can create a new world from scratch or you can join your friends to play a multi-device network.

## Netflix

Things wouldn't just be right if Netflix is not on this list. The Netflix app just seems like it was made for the Chromebook. You get a clean and smooth experience. Like you get all the menu options packaged in the menu button on the left.

## VLC

This app is a must have for your Chromebook. You can play video files that are stored locally on your Chromebooks drive. While the web based version is available in the Chrome web store, the VLC android app can find your videos immediately while the former will have you manually inputting directories.

## Pocket

One feature that Chromebook users love is its lightweight body which is easy to carry around. Also the minimalist OS is a nice feature as it focuses mainly on browsing the web.

While browsing, you might come across an interesting piece of content that you would like to read or explore, but don't have the time for it at the moment. With the Pocket app, you can save it so you can read it later when you have time. And yes, it can be done without an internet connection.

### Numeric Calculator and Converter

Yes you have the default calculator on the Chromebook, what device doesn't. But most times, they leave a lot to be desired. With the numeric calculator app, you get more than just the basics but also more advanced calculations and conversion abilities. And it works offline, no internet connection needed.

## Quik

Quik is an amazing tool that you can use to stuff photos and videos in just one clip. And you don't need to tap much. When you select your media, you can include more than 20 effects that you can find just beneath the timeline of your clip. One of these effects is Action. This mixes your images and videos with various sliders and some soundtracks. Dandy does about the same thing.

## Reddit

Unlike most apps, you don't have the Reddit app showing in full screen mode. It's like the portrait mobile screen is shown on the display. Because of some of its limitations, you are not able to use a mouse wheel and scroll content when the cursor is outside the active area. But you get the same thing as you get with Reddit.

## Slack

This is a communication service and it is invite-only. You will be provided with the server address by the company and you may have access to the chat channel list or the entire list. You get a more streamlined approach to the process with the android app.

## Spotify

With Spotify, you have access to a large music library where you'll find millions of titles that you search by the artist name, album or by the song itself. You could say this app turns your Chromebook device into a collection of hits and beats that would make you look like a DJ. You could even sing along as your favorite music plays and discover beautiful new songs that you didn't know existed.

## Tune In Radio

The only advantage that Tune In Radio has over IHeartRadio is that it covers 8 countries. IHeartRadio only covers 4. This app is also simple and clean and you don't get the huge ugly ads as you get in the web version. To view all the categories, you just have to go to the browse menu that is with the favorites and settings.

## Webcam Toy

It's a fun app, as can be guessed from the name, but also it is another great addition to the inbuilt camera of the Chromebook. You can take shots of group photos quickly and can apply dozens of effects to them. In just one click, you will be able to share them on Facebook or other social media platforms.

CHAPTER 6

# BEST TIPS AND TRICKS

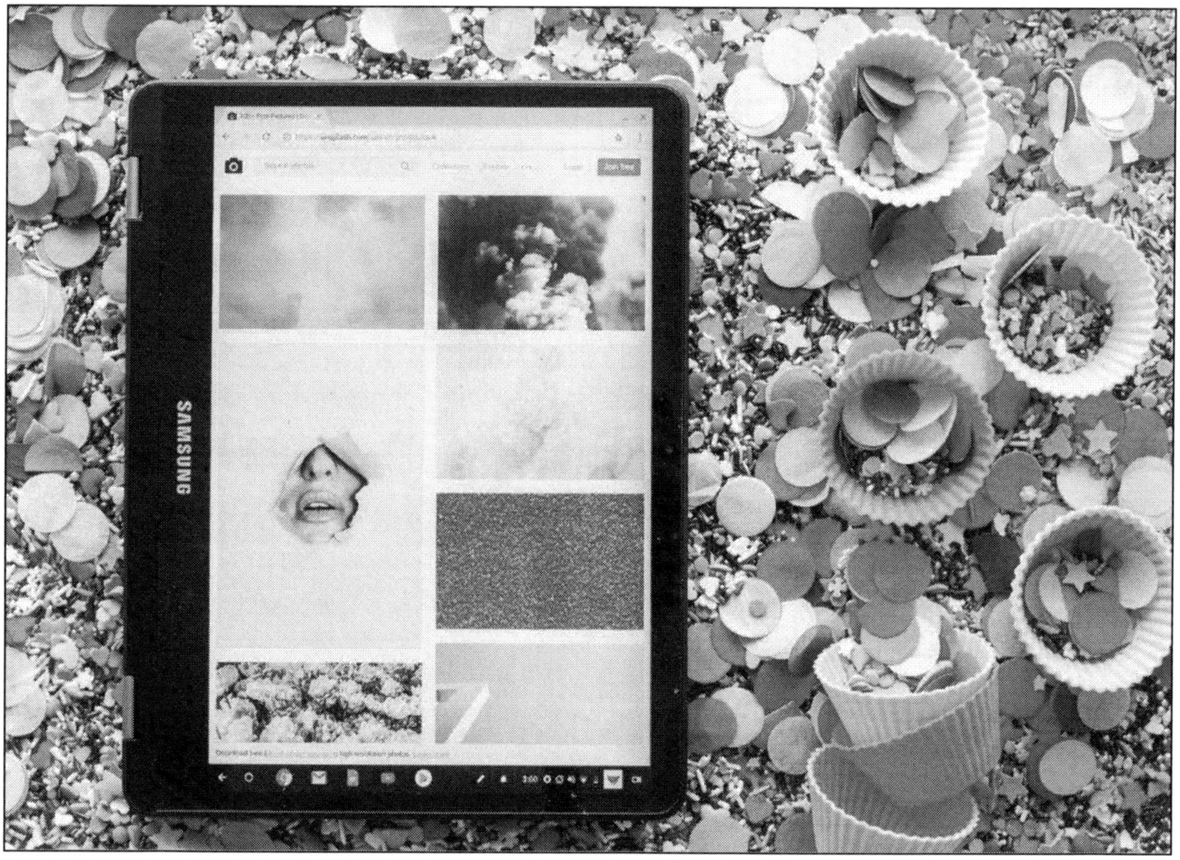


Chromebooks are preferred all over the world because they are quite simple to use. Despite the simplicity they are quite rich in features, but not all of their features are being used to their maximum potential. Chromebooks have many tips and tricks that can make them even more easy to use and interesting. This chapter will look at the best 10 Chromebook tips and tricks that you will find interesting and useful.

## Access the Overview Mode

The overview mode is a feature that allows you to see everything open on the screen at once and is just like the Expose feature on Mac. Follow these steps to access this feature on your Chromebook.

- Go to the top row of your keyboard and press the [] | | key. You can find it above the '6' button.
- You can also access the overview mode by swiping down using three fingers on your trackpad or touchscreen.
- When you access the overview mode, click on any of the available thumbnails to open that window.
- Clicking on a blank space reverts you to the previous window used.

By using this feature, you will find out that it is a good time-saver considering that you have several apps open simultaneously. Type anything to filter out the windows when you are in the Overview mode, for example, typing 'Google' will prompt your Chromebook to show Google windows that are open. This way, you will maximize your experience with your lovely gadget.

## Use Chromebook Extras

Chromebooks run on Chrome OS which makes them more than just mere computers. Chrome OS brings with it more freebies which give more value to your Chromebook with their extra functions. The moment you acquire your Chromebook and get logged in, the first thing is to visit the Chromebook Perks Page to find some awesome offers. These offers expire 60 days from the day you link your Google account with the Chromebook so you have to make full use of them before time runs out.

The offers come in the form of free games, free apps, extended subscription trials, hardware savings, and many others. They are always changing and updating from time to time. The good part of it is that there is always something for you. When you do not find a specific perk that you are looking for, you can find it by following these steps:

- Open the app Launcher and search Explore app.

- All the active Perks will be shown on the Available Perks tab.
- When you find your desired app, click on it and you will be asked to verify your eligibility.
- If available, the perk's promo code will be presented to you and you are good to go.

## Security When Sharing Your Chromebook

A Chromebook is a very private device since it is directly linked to your Google account. This means that if anyone else gains access to your account, that person can view your files, check your emails, view your photos, and access many other things. Unlike Windows-based computers, Chromebooks may not be that easy to share with someone else. However, there are situations when you need to lend it to a loved one but you do not want them to access your private files. Take advantage of the Guest Mode which allows you to gain access to most of Chrome OS features without logging into an account.

- Open the Quick Setting menu on the bottom-right corner.
- Sign out of your profile.
- To enter a temporary profile, Click Guest Mode.
- Keep in mind that the Guest Mode is only useful when you need to use apps or functions which do not require you to Log in first.

## Opening Apps Using Keys

Bearing in mind that you need apps to perform tasks on your Chromebook, finding and opening them in a quick way helps you to operate it with ease. Opening apps that are on your Chromebook's Dock or taskbar has never been this easy with the use of shortcuts. Clicking Alt + 1 opens the first app on the left of your Chromebook shelf. Pressing Alt + 2 opens the second app whereas Alt + 3 opens the third application and the chain goes on.

These shortcuts help you to search and open apps without wasting much time. You can arrange your apps starting with the most used app to the least used ones for quick access. For example, if your Shelf has Chrome as the first app, you just press Alt + 1 and you will be directed straight into the Chrome app.

## Add Restart Button on Chromebook

Chromebooks do not come with restart buttons. This means that when you want to restart your Chromebook, you have to shut it down and turn it on again which is quite boring. Given that your device encounters performance problems, for instance, graphical issues, slow performance, and mouse latency, among others, restarting it may be a good option. If this is your case, you can create a Restart button manually using the following steps.

- Press Ctrl + Shift + O, go to the top right corner, and click on the three-dot menu.
- Click Add New Bookmark and type Restart in the name field. Go to the URL field and type "chrome://restart" and save the bookmark.
- To access the bookmark easily, drag it to the bookmark bar.
- Now, when the need to restart your device instantly arises, you simply have to go to Chrome and click on the Restart bookmark.

## Chromebook Shortcuts

The use of Chromebooks has been made easy by shortcuts, which help you complete tasks quickly. This means that you no longer have to go deeper into your device's functions but rather use the keyboard to instantly open a file, complete a task, and much more. The underlisted are a few shortcuts you may find interesting and useful.

- To open a file in the browser, press Ctrl + o.
- Press Ctrl + n to open a new window.
- Press Shift + Ctrl + n to open a new window in Incognito mode.
- Press Shift + Ctrl + w to close the current window.
- To open a new tab press Ctrl + t.
- Press Ctrl + 9 to go to the last tab in the window.
- Press Ctrl + Tab to go to the next tab in the window.
- Press Alt + Right arrow to go to the next page in your device's browsing history.

- Press Alt + Left arrow to go to the previous page in the browsing history.
- Press Shift + Alt + m to open the Files app.
- Press Shift + Ctrl and + or –(minus).
- Press Ctrl + search + m or Ctrl + Launcher + m to magnify the whole screen.
- To take a screenshot, press Ctrl + Show Windows.

These are just a few of the many shortcuts available on your Chromebook. These devices are meant to be as user-friendly as possible so they have shortcuts to aid that.

## Enable Offline mode for Google Docs

Enabling the Offline mode for Google Docs and Drive is possible on Chromebook, provided you want to use it without the internet. The first step is to install Google Docs Offline Chrome extension. It allows you to do advanced copy and paste functions in Google Docs, Sheets, and Slides. This extension allows you to create, edit, and view documents, spreadsheets, images, PDFs, and presentations without the use of the internet. Make sure your device has enough space to save your files and turn on Offline access.

Once you have successfully installed the Google Docs Offline Chrome extension, you can find files saved for offline access by going to the Settings menu in your Google Drive, Sheets, or Slides app and tapping Offline. To save a file for offline views follow these steps.

- Open Google Drive.
- Next to the file, click More.
- Tap Make available offline and the file will be ready for offline use.

You can also make a document while offline by going to the Files menu and finding the option, Make available for Offline. Make sure that all these settings are updated while your Chromebook is connected to the internet.

## Reset Your Chromebook

Resetting your Chromebook is an option to consider when you are having problems with your Chrome OS. This process is called Powerwash on Chrome OS and the reset process is similar to that on Android. The only difference is that on Chrome OS, all your files are synced to Google Drive so data loss is not a thing to worry about. The following steps will guide you through the reset process.

- Open Settings, go to the left pane menu, and click Advanced.
- Go to Reset Settings and click on the Reset button.
- The Chromebook will restart and after that sign in with your Google account and everything will be back to normal just like before.

When a Chromebook has been reset, it will be refreshed thereby speeding its processes and improving its operations.

If you would like to view the shortcuts for a particular app, you just have to right click the app in the launcher. You can also long press. When you do, you'll see the list of shortcuts for that particular app.

## Reach the Launcher Fast

If you are using the Chromebook in tablet mode, there's this feature that you would like to try out. It’s the feature to access the launcher fast. All you need to do is swipe upwards from an area that’s empty at the lower part of the display

## Clear all Notifications

Let's say you get too many notifications, as is often the case, and you’d like to clean them up. It’s easy. If you use an android device, you will be familiar with the button to clear all notifications. This is a cool option and it’s also available in the Chromebook. When you are in the notification screen, just scroll to the very bottom of the notification and choose the button for Clear All.

## Get To the Quick Setting

Just like android, there is the notification panel and also the option for quick settings. If you would like to access the quick settings, you can find it at the lower right corner. But you can reach it quick with Shift + Alt + N

### Lock Screen Note Taking

If you would like to take notes from the lock screen of the Chromebook:

- Install the Google keep android app
- Go to settings in the app
- In stylus, turn on the lock screen note taking option

### Transfer to the Cloud Immediately

Yes the Chromebook has inbuilt storage. But let's face it, this wouldn't last you long. And if it does, it's only because you manage the space. But you don't want to manage your experience on your laptop. You want to enjoy it, is that not so?

That's why we have Google Drive. This will allow you to be able to send whatever files you've got straight to the cloud. And the best part of this is that when you download something from Chrome, you are given the option to save it directly to the cloud.

If you want to use the feature on your Chromebook, this is how you go about enabling it:

- Go to Settings.
- Choose Show Advanced Settings.
- If you look beneath the download option, you will see options for Change.
- Depending on your preferences, you can just choose Google Drive. Or if you would like you can select the folder inside your Google Drive.
- Choose Open
- Return to these settings screen. Find the option that says Ask Where to Save Each File before Downloading. When you find it, uncheck the checkbox.

Now if you download a file you will have the option to save it straight to Google Drive

## Keep the Shelf Hidden

If you check the bottom part of the screen on your Chromebook, you'll find a row of apps that displays the favorites. This is what is called the Shelf. And if you want, you can hide it.

- Right-click the shelf
- Choose the option for Auto hide

### Calculate With the Launcher

A lot can be done with the launcher. And one of its features is the Calculator. This can help you do basic calculations like '7834/467'. You can also get the option of Converter that can help you with stuff like '47 feet into meters'.

### Sync with Your Smartphone

If you have an Android device and you have your Google account logged in from here, you can sync it to your Chromebook. What I mean is that your Android device will be connected to your Chromebook as long as it is on the same account. So when you search for something on the device, you would see the title or suggestions appear if you've searched for it before.

## Open a Shelf App Quickly

If you have an app in the shelf, you don't have to go looking for it on a desktop screen or anywhere else. You can use a shortcut to open it right from a shelf. This will come in handy if you're multitasking. All you have to do is press the Alt key and the number that corresponds to the item on the shelf. What I mean is that if Google Chrome is number 5 on the shelf, you just need to press Alt + 5

## Quickly Open Links in Another Tab

If you want to open a link in a new tab on your Chromebook, there's a faster way that you can go about it. And I mean much faster. All you need to do is to use three fingers to click the link on the trackpad and the link will be opened in a new tab. This is great news as without this shortcut, you would have to right click the link and the press new tab

## Close Tabs with Ease

Here's another trick that requires using 3 fingers. If you would like to close a tab, you could just do so easily by going to the title bar and clicking with 3 fingers on the trackpad.

## Open Windows in a Snap

So you are making use of the chrome browser, but then the window is filled with many open tabs. Your next option is to open a new window and leave the previous window to be crowded. To do this easily, press Ctrl + N and a new window will be opened.

### Add Most Used Site to Shelf

If there's a website that you regularly visit, you can add it on the shelf of your device so that you can access it easily and quickly.

- Open the Chrome Menu, when the site is open
- Choose More Tools
- Hit the option for Create Shortcut
- Sign In To Restricted Sites

Some websites do not view the Chromebook as a real computer. Every organization has its own rules.

As a result of this, you will not be allowed to sign in to the website and make use of its functions. Fine, they can do whatever they want as long as we've got User Agent Switcher.

Now what in the world is that? It's just an extension that you can install on your Chromebook. When you enter the menu of that extension, select another operating system and voila!

The website is smart but not smart enough to figure out what you are doing. It will be tricked to think that you aren't using the Chromebook device, but another operating system. And with that you'll be able to use the site.

## Undersize the Keyboard

There's this real estate keyboard that comes with your Chromebook by default. You'll find it when your device is in tablet mode. You can make use of it if you like to. But for some, the keyboard might be too wide out to handle. You can reduce it instead. Hit the second icon that's at the top row of the screen's keyboard. This is the icon that has a black rectangle embedded inside another rectangle. This action will shrink the on screen keyboard to the distant side. Like the size you find on your smartphone. And depending on where you will like the keyboard to sit, you can move it around. Just use the icon.

## Write With Hand

If you are more interested in using handwriting for your keyboard, you can use the icon that's at the first place on the top row of the Chromebook's keyboard. The icon looks like a squiggle drawn by hand.

When you select it, you'll see the canvas open. It is from here that you are able to write whatever you would like to write. You could use a stylus or a finger to write this, though the stylus is preferable. As you write, it will be changed to texts.

CHAPTER 7

# MAINTENANCE, BATTERY, UPDATES AND DIAGNOSTIC

Chromebooks, unlike most laptops, are also simple to maintain and reasonably inexpensive. Your computers' efficiency and functionality, like any other technology, can suffer if they're not properly preserved for long periods of time. The first thing you should do before storing your gadgets is make sure their battery level is at least 80% charged. This means that if your machines are kept unplugged for an extended period of time, they should not run out of power.

Remember that you don't need to entirely unplug the battery from the Chromebook for effective maintenance. Instead, plug in the computer and simultaneously press the "Refresh" and "power" buttons. The battery will be disconnected. If the disconnect was successful, you shouldn't be able to turn the machine on even if you have a good charge.

Maintaining your Chromebooks this way may seem inconvenient initially, but that is one of the greatest ways to maintain their longevity. This will limit battery discharge and keep your battery life from being harmed by frequent charge and discharge rates. If you can't get your Chromebook to the battery detach condition, you may still protect your gadget by disconnecting the charging wire and storing it somewhere dry and cool.

## Battery Care for Chromebooks

One of your Chromebook's most important characteristics is the battery. Many educators choose Chromebooks because of how long they can operate on battery power before charging. Even the greatest batteries, however, do not last indefinitely. The length of time a Chromebook may run between charges may begin to diminish based on your adherence to Chromebook upkeep. Chromebooks are incredibly sturdy and robust since they use lithium batteries. However, these devices can be damaged while being stored. To ensure that your Chromebook investment lasts as long as possible, keep the following rules in mind:

Over the summer, don't let the battery completely drain. Before putting the device away, be sure it's fully charged and turned off. A battery can be severely damaged if it is left to drain for a long time.

A Chromebook should not be left plugged in. Leaving your smartphone hooked into a charger or cart for weeks or months diminishes battery life and raises the chance of various problems.

Before storing your Chromebook, turn it off. Making sure the device is properly shut down before storage is an important part of excellent Chromebook maintenance. If you simply close the lid after each usage, the screen will finally turn off in this instance, and the gadget will enter standby mode. While standby only consumes a minimal amount of energy, it nevertheless requires ongoing energy. If you don't want your battery to be drained, make sure your machines are completely turned off. Press and hold the Chromebook's power button till the screen goes black. To confirm that your gadget is entirely shut off, the screen should remain blank when you release the power switch. You can start storing the machines once they are entirely shut off.

## How To Store It

You must make sure that there are no more than 7 Chromebooks stacked on top of each other. The heaviness of the gadgets may cause the displays to fracture.

Keeping your Chromebooks out of the way of cleaners and foot traffic is a good idea. This should lessen the chances of them falling over.

You should keep your Chromebooks in a cool, dry place away from direct sunlight.

## Updating Chrome

Chromebooks are one of the best options because of their great built-in security, integrated encryption features, and specialized hardware. That's why they're popular with schools and other groups. Make sure your Chromebook is up to date; otherwise, security features, as well as other key quality-of-life enhancements will begin to lag. If you wait too long, you may lose access to Google Cloud.

## Access Settings

When a new version of the operating system is released, your Chromebook will automatically update in most circumstances. However, this may not always work, or you may want to double-check the update in these circumstances. Here's how to get started.

Check that a particular patch has been applied. Make sure your Chromebook is turned on and linked to the internet. On Chrome OS, look down at the taskbar and to the right, you should see the System Tray, which contains the clock. To continue, select the clock.

With the System Tray open, tap the gear-shaped Settings icon from the icons at the top of the window.

Check for New Information.

To check for new information, he settings menu will open, displaying information about your network connections. Look in the lower-left section and pick the final item on the left menu, About Chrome OS, to learn more about your updates.

The Chromebook will now provide information about your Chrome OS version. Select the Check for Updates button on the far right.

If an update is detected, your Chromebook should begin upgrading automatically at this point. Here is what you should do:

Allow time for the update to download. The percentage of the update that has been completed is displayed under Google Chrome OS. It's critical that your Chromebook doesn't shut off suddenly at this time, so make sure it's plugged in if necessary.

Once the download is complete, you'll be prompted to restart your computer to finalize the update. Make sure you don't have any work to save before selecting Restart. It may take several minutes for Chrome OS to restart when the operation is completed.

If it was a major update, navigate to the Google Chrome OS section and pick See What's New from the drop-down menu. This will show you any new features that have recently been added to Chrome OS.

## Powerwash

It's sometimes great to have a fresh start. You may simply wipe the slate completely and start again with your Chromebook. When you have a lot of garbage on your smartphone, you could find this beneficial. If you wish to reset your Chromebook to its default configuration if you're giving it to someone else. With Chromebook's built-in Powerwash feature, you can wipe your device speedily, easily, and safely. Sign in to your Chromebook and perform the following steps to powerwash it:

- Open the Shelf's Settings panel and select Settings.
- Select Show Advanced Settings towards the end of the screen.
- In the Powerwash section at the bottom of the screen, click the Powerwash button.
- A dialog box displays, informing you that you must restart.
- Click the Restart option if you're certain you would like to wipe your Chromebook clean.

You can't undo power washing like you can't undo breaking an egg. Your Chromebook transforms into a safe, power-cleaning machine after you click Restart. Nothing will be left on the device. The good news is that nothing on your Google Drive or other web services will be affected.

## Recovery

You can recover your Chromebook's operating system (OS) if it isn't working properly. The recovery process involves deleting and reinstalling the operating system. Backup files if possible before recovering your Chromebook.

- Recover is necessary under the following circumstances:
- If you've tried other troubleshooting methods but nothing has worked.
- When you've asked the professionals in your Chromebook assistance forum for advice, they've suggested that you recover.
- After trying less invasive methods before you recuperate.
- When you have tried turning off your Chromebook and then on again.

## The Recovery Process

Remove any devices that are attached to your Chromebook, including a mouse or an external hard drive. Hold down Esc + Refresh for a few seconds, then Power. Power must be relinquished. Some Chromebook models include: Press Esc + Maximize for a few seconds, then push Power. Let go of the other keys when a message appears on the screen. Turn off Chromebox first. With a paper clip or similar instrument, press the recovery button. Press the Power button to turn the Chromebox back on. Once you see a message on the screen, release the recovery button.

## Traditional Recovery

To run the traditional recovery process on your Chromebook, follow these easy steps:

Install Google Chrome.

Install the extension for recovery. To access the recovery extension, click Extensions in the top right corner of your browser window. The Chromebook Recovery Utility extension should be selected. Make sure the extension popup is turned on if it doesn't appear on your screen automatically.

Start the recovery process. To begin, select Get started. On the Chromebook with the problem, select Recover using external disk and follow the on-screen instructions.

CHAPTER 8

# FAQS AND TROUBLESHOOTING COMMON PROBLEMS

Fortunately, your Chromebook is built to last. According to Google, any Chromebook device is expected to last 5 years from the release date. Take note: the lifespan counts from the date of release, not the date of purchase. During this design lifespan, your Chromebook can receive all Chrome OS support.

Ideally, nothing goes wrong with your machine because it continues to be updated by default. But if anything goes wrong, there are ways of fixing it. Unfortunately, we cannot list all the things that can go wrong. But based on users' experience over time, there've been hardware challenges like battery not charging; Bluetooth refusing to work; camera refusing to launch or capture; keyboard doesn't work, plus problems related to the touchpad, touchscreen and monitor not being able to connect.

The second class of problems that have been reported over time has to do with the Operating System. They include Chromebook crashing, freezing, or being too slow; or it turns off and on endlessly; or the system won't turn on, run update, or charge.

Take note: these problems don't occur often, and when they do, there are online walkthroughs that you can follow to fix them. You find them under Google Help. But if you try all suggested steps to no avail, you're advised to contact your Google Chromebook maker for the solution. They're ever ready to help you out.

## Chromebook Troubleshooting

As you use your Chromebook device, it's almost a certainty that you will face one problem or the other on the device. If you ever face trouble using the Chromebook, this part has got your covered. Here are some of the major problems that users of the Chromebook face and that you may be currently experiencing.

And it doesn't just stop there, there's also going to be solutions to how you can fight the problems. But there's something that you may want to keep in mind. The Chrome OS is centered on web apps. As a result, you might not be clear about the difference between Chrome OS and the Chrome browser. But you should know that they are not the same thing.

### Chrome OS runs too slow

If you happen to see the Chrome OS operating very slowly, the best thing to do will be to restart it. You should also try to check if a system update is available. For most, the devices will check for updates and download automatically when it's connected to Wi-Fi.

But you can still check if things are in place by

- Selecting the time area that is on the lower right
- Select Settings
- Choose the Menu
- Hit About Chrome OVS
- Then you will select Check For Updates. This will then check if there is any new update available

**Chrome wouldn't stop shutting down and restarting by itself**

To be clear, this is a serious problem that users face. Serious because it just means that there is a problem with the OS. If you see this happening to your device, you will have to recover your Chromebook fully and, well, that's no easy task. With recovery, you will have much of your data saved from the OS.

To do this, you will need to have not only your Chromebook, but another computer as well. The other computer should be able to access the Chrome browser. It should also have a USB and SD drive. When that is done, then you want to download the Chromebook Recovery Utility on that second computer. The extension will take you through the whole process.

Open it up, and you will be prompted to make a recovery media. This will be used to transfer data and settings temporarily, you just have to follow the instructions and make use of your storage device to transfer settings into the Chromebook utility. Then you reset your Chromebook fully.

## Received error messages after updating the Chrome OS

If you are experiencing this, you can solve it by checking the internet connection. You want to have a Wi-Fi connection that is strong (or Ethernet). You also want to keep a warning in mind: make sure that you are not updating over data connection. This will eat through the monthly data and it could probably be the reason why you get the error messages.

Another thing that you can do to help is restarting your Chromebook. You just have to press the power button for you to shut it down. That is after you have made sure that you're done with all of your existing work. When Chromebook is shut down fully, use the power button to restart the device. This can help to deal with some of the errors in updating.

## Downloading an important update but it will not work

Have you been trying to download the same type of update many times but it doesn't work? Then that just means that you will need to reboot the Chromebook device. If you want to go through this the easy route, then you will just need to press the power button the Chromebook to turn if off then press it to turn it back on again.

If you've done that but didn't it work, then you will need to sign out of your Chromebook account. When you are signed out, you will reset your Chromebook. This will then clear all the settings and the hard drive content. Since everything will be wiped, you will want to make sure that you save to the Cloud.

- If you have already saved to the Cloud and want to restart, you just have to
- Press Ctrl + Alt + Shift + R.
- Now a box should show up, when it does, select the Restart option.
- Choose the option for Powerwash
- Hit Continue

### When I sign into Chrome OS, I get errors

You may get quite a lot of error messages when you try to sign into your Chrome OS device. Instead of you going through them one by one, you may want to check the walkthrough that has been provided by Google. Find the solution to help with dealing with errors like this.

But still, you want to do a quick double check of your password, Google account and also of your username. Be sure that they are all up to date and working as they are supposed to. Many times, the problem sprouts from either of these credentials.

## The browser tabs continues to reload and load slowly

It's not a new problem for the Chrome OS to run into problems regarding the browser tabs. The tabs just keep reloading without end and every other thing just slow down. To be sure, the guiltiest fellow is the memory. You may be running low on memory. So the fix is for you to close down any of the tabs that you really don't need and quit multitasking.

Then you try to load the tabs and see if it changes for the better. This can also happen to many programs and apps. You can just press Shift + Escape. This will then open up the Task Manager. The Task Manager reveals all the applications that are used currently. If there's an app that seems strange or that you don't need, just close it.

### The Chrome OS crashes for no reason

Something that some users face with their Chromebook device is that it suddenly crashes as they try to browse the web. When this happens, your go to option should be to turn off your Chromebook device and put it back on.

If you do that and there's no improvement, then the problem could be with the webpage. If you want to fix this, then you will need to quit all of the apps. Then press Ctrl + Shift + R to do a hard refresh. Another thing that you can try is doing a hard reset. You will just need to press and hold the power key.

Another cause for the issue could be with the extensions or some apps. To solve the problem, you can try to take them away. If you would have to remove an app,

- Select the Launcher
- Click the Up Arrow
- Right click on the app that you would to remove
- Choose either Remove from Chrome or Uninstall
- If you would have to uninstall an extension, then you would need to
- Launch Chrome
- Select More
- Then choose More Tools
- Select Extensions

When the extensions show up, then hit the Remove option beside the extension that you would like to remove.

If you don't want to remove the extension, you can also try to disable it. You just go through the same previous steps but instead of uninstalling, you just turn it off.

**Tried to load web pages but shows error messages**

When you try to load a web page with Chrome and it can't load it properly, you will get the error message that says 'aw snap'. What this means is that the web page did its best load but didn't get far enough and crashed. If this happens once, maybe it's just the site.

But if it happens regularly, then you have 2 main things to accuse; your settings or the operating system. One easy thing that you do to solve the problem is to close all the open tabs and windows. If you try to close some tabs and you get the chance to open a new one, then you have gotten to the limit of the device's RAM.

- Another thing to check out are faulty extensions. If you want to solve this issue
- Go to the Main Menu (it's the menu with many horizontal lines)
- Choose More Tools
- Move to Extensions

Now you want to uncheck the extensions. It's good to uncheck all of them.

Now try and see if your problem is solved. If everything works fine, then you will need to set time aside. Enable an extension, reload to see if the page loads correctly. When you enable an extension and things start to get wonky, then you know that's the guilty one, serve him justice.

If you tried everything and nothing seems to work, then you will want to check your internet connection. You can also clear your cache. And yes, try to load the webpage in incognito mode.

## Chrome OS continues to say that webpage is not available

This error, most times, is caused by issues with proxy or cookie. But you actually want to check if you got the web address correct. If it's the cookie that is the issue, then you will need to delete all of them. To do this,

- Select the time at the lower right
- Choose Settings
- Select Advanced
- Move over to the Privacy section
- Then you choose Content Settings

Now you'll have the power to delete different browser data that you would like to delete.

## Choose the option for All Cookie and Site Data.

Select Remove All. Before you do this, you might want to make sure that you have saved the online passwords.

For the problem of proxy, you might see a message about issues of proxy. You may need to change the proxy settings. But don't touch anything if you have no idea what to do. One great fix to do here is to,

- Select the time at the bottom
- Choose Settings
- Enter the section for Internet Connection

You now want to find the option for Allow Proxies For Shared Networks. Check the box belonging to it.

If you are making use of the guest profile provision in the Chromebook, then this should solve the issue. But just know that you will need to enter in the correct setting for the proxy after you check the box. Continue if you know what you are doing.

**Can't connect to a strong Wi-Fi network**

If you're having trouble connecting to a strong Wi-Fi network on your Chromebook, there are several troubleshooting steps you can follow to resolve the issue. First, ensure that your Chromebook's Wi-Fi is turned on by clicking on the network icon located in the bottom-right corner of the screen and selecting the Wi-Fi option. Next, select the network you want to connect to from the list of available networks and enter the password if prompted. If you're still unable to connect, try restarting your Chromebook and router, as this can often resolve connectivity issues. Additionally, you can try forgetting the network and then reconnecting to it by clicking on the network icon, selecting the Wi-Fi network, and choosing "Forget." Afterward, attempt to reconnect by selecting the network again and entering the password. If the problem persists, you can try resetting your network settings by going to Settings > Advanced > Reset settings > Reset network. This will reset all network settings to their default values, which may resolve any underlying issues. If you're still unable to connect, consider contacting your internet service provider for further assistance. As for shortcut keys, you can quickly access network settings by pressing the Alt + Shift + S keys simultaneously, allowing you to troubleshoot network connectivity more efficiently.

# CONCLUSION

Thanks for reading this book! If you're a Senior looking for assistance to use your Chromebook well, use it safely, or keep it in good condition, you can join the conversation. The tone is simple so you can easily understand and follow the steps. Chromebooks are simple, and there's no reason to prepare a complicated manual that confuses the user.

The Chromebook was produced to make your life easier, and you should learn to take advantage of all its features. But the question is: How do you take total control of your Chromebook and over-utilize it? This book was written to answer these questions and many more which are often encountered by seniors. Take your time and enjoy the specially-prepared tips and tricks to make using your device a real pleasure.

Remember, this isn't a literary work to read from cover to cover and keep aside. Nor is it intended to be studied like a textbook upon which you'd write a test. A user guide is more like a cookbook. It's kept handy and consulted for new recipes, or to remind yourself of cooking tips you already know, just to ensure you're doing things right. Take note of how certain problems you may encounter using the Chromebook are highlighted in this book.

All the best as you start using your Google Chromebook!

Made in United States
Troutdale, OR
11/03/2026

56847408R00044